1 MONTH OF
FREE
READING

at

www.ForgottenBooks.com

By purchasing this book you are
eligible for one month membership to
ForgottenBooks.com, giving you
unlimited access to our entire
collection of over 1,000,000 titles via
our web site and mobile apps.

To claim your free month visit:
www.forgottenbooks.com/free890047

ISBN 978-0-266-79205-5
PIBN 10890047

FEATURES

DEPARTMENTS

ON THE COVERS

ON THE COVER: Just a seagull over a stormy sea? Perhaps it represents a Dove of Peace above a troubled Earth; even a partridge looking for a pear tree. Photo by Jim Couch.

ON THE BACK COVER: Georgia's State Bird, the Brown Thrasher, and State Flower, the Cherokee Rose, as commissioned by the Atlanta Audubon Society, and depicted by artist Richard A. Parks of Atlanta. The original was recently presented to the State of Georgia for the Governor's Mansion and was accepted by Governor Carter. Prints suitable for framing (16 x 20) are available from the Atlanta Audubon Society.

Outdoors
in georgia

December 1972   Volume 1   Number 6

Outdoors in Georgia is the official monthly magazine of the Georgia Department of Natural Resources, published at the Department's offices, Trinity-Washington Building, 270 Washington St., Atlanta, Georgia 30334. No advertising accepted. Subscriptions are $3 for one year or $6 for three years. Printed by Williams Printing Company, Atlanta, Ga. Notification of address change must include old address label from a recent magazine, new address and ZIP code, with 30 days notice. No subscription requests will be accepted without ZIP code. Articles and photographs may be reprinted when proper credit given. Contributions are welcome, but the editors assume no responsibility or liability for loss or damage of articles, photographs, or illustrations, Second-class postage paid at Atlanta, Ga.

MAGAZINE STAFF
Phone 656-3530

H. E. (Bud) Van Orden
Editor-in-Chief

Bob Wilson
Editor

Staff Writers	**Art Director**	**Staff Photographers**
Dick Davis	Liz Carmichael Jones	Jim Couch
Aaron Pass		Bob Busby
T. Craig Martin		

Linda Wayne
Circulation Manager

Whoops—
And Then It Was Too Late

It happens every year, and it shouldn't. A simple apology doesn't make it right. What's even more disheartening, had the outdoorsman extended the common courtesy to check before he cast, or look before he pulled the trigger, perhaps his longtime fishing buddy would not have that long scar on his face, or his neighbor's son would still be alive.

Yes, it happens every year, and tragically, it has already happened this hunting and fishing season in Georgia.

Courtesy, ethics, common sense, mutual trust, call it whatever you like; it all boils down to the same thing. We must respect the rights of others to enjoy and participate in outdoor sporting activities, and to do so without constantly being on guard for the thoughtless, irresponsible sportsman who thinks only of himself and whose philosophy is let the others beware.

Enjoying the first days of deer season a hunter hears the gentle noise of foilage being brushed and sees the leaves of a bush begin to move not knowing if caused by man or beast, but yet he fires—*whoops,* and then it's too late.

An angler in the north Georgia mountains, vying for the taste of fresh trout, whips his cast without first checking to see if others are in the area and snags the hand of a nearby fisherman—*whoops,* and then it's too late.

The wake of a boating enthusiast checking to see how fast his new motor can make his boat skim the waters is just large enough to overturn a small rowboat and dump a father and his young son overboard—*whoops,* and then it's too late.

Property is posted. It is even fenced, but continuously the second and third strand of the barbed wire is held apart as trespassers look for new areas to camp, hunt, hike or picnic without the property owner's permission, in violation of state law—*whoops,* and then it's too late.

Stories like these are not the exception among Georgia's outdoorsmen, but occur with alarming regularity. Perhaps the answer is too simple. Respect for the rights of others so that all of our outdoor activities can be enjoyed to their fullest without constant fear of loss of life or limb is the ideal image that we must strive to build. Knowing that others care as much as you in the care, preservation and conservation of our natural resources will mean that our natural resources will be around a lot longer for all to enjoy. Real sportsmen and outdoorsmen don't have to be told for they already respect the rights of others and know the meaning of practicing good outdoor manners and conservation principles.

However, if some sportsmen continually fail to practice good rules of outdoor ethics and a proper code of conduct and respect for others when in the outdoors of Georgia, all too soon they may hear themselves saying *whoops,* but by then it will be to no avail, for just as in all the other instances it will be too late.

Bud Van Orden

Power Enough?

By Aaron Pass

What hunter has not, at some time or another, felt that sick, sinking feeling in the pit of his stomach as he confronts the bitter realization that he would not recover a wounded animal. The loss of wounded game is one of the most disturbing and disappointing experiences that a true sportsman can endure, and such an occurrence is almost sure to spoil an otherwise perfect day afield. It is hard to put the full emotional impact of this situation into words that adequately explain the feeling.

There is, of course, the somewhat selfish feeling of wasted game that will not grace the family dinner table, but there are other, deeper disappointments. One is the ego-galling reflection on the hunter's ability and competence, particularly if there had been any questionable judgment involved in the taking of the shot. Ultimately though, there is the feeling of betrayal one must feel out of respect for the wounded animal in the sense that the "Predatory Contract" has been violated. The hunter/predator has failed to accomplish his self-ordained role of cleanly harvesting his prey.

Contrary to the well publicized opinions of the vocal anti-hunting groups, most hunters get no psychic thrill from maiming or needlessly inflicting pain on animals. True hunters do seek to kill their game as any predator seeks to kill his prey, but an equal goal of the hunting code of ethics is that it be done efficiently and quickly.

That game is wounded and eventually lost is a painful truth to relate, particularly in view of the fact that such instances tend to verify the allegations that hunters are little better than bloodthirsty psychotics. If hunting is to survive as a legal sport, it is going to become necessary for each of us to adhere more firmly in reality to the principles of good sportsmanship we shout in public.

—AFP

One of the most difficult and certainly one of the most controversial problems in wildlife management is the regulation of rifle calibers and cartridges used for big game hunting. Sporting ethics and humane considerations aside for the moment, the continued utilization and enjoyment of our wild game resources is becoming increasingly dependent on the more efficient production and harvest of these resources on a constantly decreasing amount of usable land. Undeniably, it is grossly inefficient to lose wounded game as a result of inadequate and underpowered armament used in otherwise regulated hunting. It is also a fact that there are a good many centerfire rifle cartridges (and all rimfires) on the market that will not reliably or humanely kill big game under normal hunting conditions. Nevertheless, there seems to be a significant number of individuals who, lacking good sense and/or scruples, would use these undersize cartridges to hunt, and ultimately to wound and waste game. If a state wildlife agency attempts to rectify this situation by means of establishing minimum legal power standards for big game cartridges, enraged outcry is often raised by a few members of the hunting public.

The choice of a hunting weapon is, like the choice of a good friend, an intimate and personal thing and is as strongly defended as the right to hunt. The bond between a hunter and his gun existed long before D. Boone christened his favorite flintlock with a pet name, and if state regulation crosses that bond it has stopped preaching and started meddling. "After all," the sentiment goes, "Grandad killed many a deer and bear with this old .32-20, so who are the state game and fish bureaucrats to tell me it doesn't have enough power."

Unfortunately there is just enough truth to this brand of reasoning to make it most difficult to prove the aforementioned .32-20 inadequate for deer-size game. Grandad undoubtedly did slay gobs of game with this vencrable and feeble old cartridge; just as the earliest men slugged it out with mammoths using stone-tipped lances and carefully dropped boulders. In both cases they were underarmed, but the hunters had little other choice in their respective eras.

Deer are not particularly difficult to kill and virtually any rifle cartridge will do the job if all the variables are controlled. Even the diminutive .22 rimfire short will bowl them over like nobody's business if the deer is still and unexcited, within proper range (very close) and the tiny bullet is placed exactly right (in the brain, preferably through the eye). A thoroughly spooked buck, pumped full of adrenalin, bolting through the brush a hundred yards away is quite a different situation, however.

This brings us to a couple of bitter realities the modern deer hunter will have to face. Firstly, Grandad usually waited for a better shot than the one just described, since the farm wouldn't fire him if he wasn't back by Monday. Secondly, to be painfully blunt, Grandson is not often as good a shot as the old man was.

Due to the fact that many hunters must take shots which are a far cry from the classic, stock-still, out-in-the open broadside pose that deer strike for the cover of *Field & Stream*, and that most hunters simply aren't good enough shots to perfectly place the bullet under difficult conditions, most state wildlife agencies have placed minimum power restrictions on the firearms used for big game hunting. To enact such regulations takes no small amount of bravery since there is always a sizeable contingent of individuals who get upset with this restriction. They consider it their God-given prerogative as free

Many hunters are confused by regulations outlawing the .30 caliber M-1 carbine for deer hunting, because the M-1 rifle (Garand) is legal, as are many other .30 caliber cartridges. The M-1 carbine was designed to be issued in lieu of a pistol for defensive purposes and used a small cartridge (left). The M-1 rifle (Garand) is a full-sized rifle using the well known .30/06 cartridge (right). The carbine round produces less than 1000 ft. lbs. of muzzle energy and will not reliably kill deer-sized animals.

men to hunt deer with any cartridge they choose, no matter how underpowered it is.

In any attempt to establish a "minimum legal power" regulation for deer (or any other big game animal) there must be a defined and measurable standard by which all cartridges can be judged. Ideally, this standard would be killing power and be defined in terms of cartridge power, the size of the animal, and the ability of that particular cartridge to kill an animal of specified dimensions. Adequate killing power would, of course, be that level of power necessary to quickly and efficiently dispatch the animal. Killing power is relatively simple to define, but it is something else to measure. Due to a great many uncontrolled variables including condition of the animal, range, bullet construction and performance, and placement of the bullet, killing power cannot be precisely measured.

There are several measurable ballistic factors which can be used to approximate killing power and to establish an arbitrary standard of minimum performance. Velocity of the bullet, usually measured in feet-per-second (f.p.s.), and the weight of the bullet are both definitely related to killing power. By combining these known values and applying algebraic formula V^2 x Wt. divided by 450,250, bullet energy can be computed in terms of energy units known as foot-pounds. The bullet energy has a very definite proportional relationship to the real killing power of the cartridge and establishes a readily available graduated standard.

Ultimately, the minimum legal cartridge regulation is developed by trained wildlife biologists and experienced hunters who in their collective years in the field have observed first-hand the capabilities of many cartridges, both good and bad, on game

animals. By the application of these observations to a known energy standard, the capabilities of any cartridge with published figures can be reliably assessed. The resulting regulation specifying minimum legal calibers and cartridges provides the hunter with a guideline for caliber selection by which he can reasonably be assured of a clean and humane kill if he does his job and puts the bullet in the right spot.

In Georgia the minimum legal power regulation for rifle limits the deer hunter to ". . . any rifle using a centerfire cartridge with expanding bullet that is commercially available and rated at a minimum of 1100 foot pounds of muzzle energy." This regulation uses projectile (bullet) energy as the main criteria for judging adequacy for deer-sized game. The regulation also makes other attempts to further control legal deer cartridges by specifying that they must be centerfire. The portion which refers to "commercially available" does not prohibit handloaded cartridges, but does limit the handloads to cartridges which are commercially loaded above the legal minimum.

The restriction on projectiles which limits them to expanding bullets only is an extremely important one for the hunter. Proper bullet selection for the game hunted and proper bullet performance on impact is the key to efficient utilization of a cartridge's killing power, and one-shot kills.

The modern centerfire rifle cartridge normally used for big game hunting uses an expanding bullet consisting of a lead core partially covered by a protective jacket of harder metal, usually copper. The lead core is exposed at the "nose" and begins expanding when the bullet strikes something. The jacket protects the soft lead from heat generated by the friction and stresses of high velocity and controls the bullet's expansion upon impact. The bullet's killing power occurs upon impact at high velocity when the bullet's energy is suddenly and violently released in the animal's body. This violent energy release results in massive tissue destruction which creates a wound channel along the path of the bullet and a terrific infusion of hydrostatic shock through the animal. It is in this process that the expanding bullet plays a dual role. Obviously, the larger the bullet the

ONE GIFT...FOR MANY OCCASIONS THAT LASTS ALL YEAR

Birthdays. Anniversaries. Father's Day. Any Day. OUTDOORS IN GEORGIA is the ideal gift for your favorite sportsman . . . every issue is packed with features of interest to Georgia outdoorsmen.

You can order it now for any gift occasion during the year, and we'll send a letter of acknowledgment in your name. Simply fill out the blanks on the reverse side. We'll do the rest.

1 year (12 issues) $3.00
2 years (24 issues) $5.00
Special Bargain Rate: 3 years (36 issues) . . $6.00

Give the Gift that Lasts All Year . . .
Give OUTDOORS IN GEORGIA

Name _____

Address _____

City _____ State _____ Zip Code _____

I wish to subscribe for

☐ 1 year—$3.00   ☐ 2 years—$5.00   ☐ 3 years—$6.00

☐ Renewal. Please send old address label.

☐ My check is enclosed for $

    Make payable to Department of Natural Resources

☐ If moved, please include old label or former address in space below.

Address _____

City _____ State _____ Zip Code _____

PLEASE ENTER GIFT SUBSCRIPTIONS FOR:
(please print)

Name _____

Address _____

City _____ State _____ Zip Code _____

☐ 1 year—$3.00   ☐ 2 years—$5.00   ☐ 3 years—$6.00

Name _____

Address _____

City _____ State _____ Zip Code _____

☐ 1 year—$3.00   ☐ 2 years—$5.00   ☐ 3 years—$6.00

Name _____

Address _____

City _____ State _____ Zip Code _____

☐ 1 year—$3.00   ☐ 2 years—$5.00   ☐ 3 years—$6.00

larger the wound, but the expansion also slows the bullet down during its passage through the body allowing for a longer interval of energy release.

It is here that bullet construction must be evaluated in regard to the animal's size. If the bullet is too heavily constructed it will pierce the animal's body causing a narrow wound channel and releasing little of its energy. Such wounds are often eventually fatal but usually do not put the animal down on the spot and may allow it to escape. Military ammunition is particularly bad in this respect, since the bullets are fully encased in metal and do not expand at all. On the other hand, bullets which are too lightly constructed may expand too rapidly and not penetrate deeply enough to reach a vital area.

Bullet placement is the single greatest uncontrolled variable in the assessment of a cartridge's killing power. In order for any bullet to do the job it must be put in a vital spot, and just about any bullet, regardless of its power, put in a non-vital spot results in a wounded deer that may be lost.

On the other end of the scale are those hunters who try to overpower themselves with gun to make up for poor shooting. They figure that they can hit a deer just about any place and drop him in his tracks, but it just ain't so. A small white-tailed deer can carry a surprising amount of lead when it's put in the wrong spot. Even a hit in some of the right spots from some of the big magnums may allow a small deer to escape. Following the theory of big bullet game, most loading companies deduce that the bigger calibers and the heaviest bullet weights in many common calibers are to be used on the larger species of North American game. When one of these bullets, which are designed to punch through both shoulders of a 1400 lb. Moose, hits the fragile rib cage of a 150 lb. white-tail it goes on through while expanding very little, and the result can be one that "Got away."

The minimum legal power regulations are designed to eliminate those cartridges which are inadequate to efficiently kill the game. There is no guarantee, however, that using a more powerful gun will result in a sure kill. No cartridge is more adequate than the shooter behind the gun, and the responsibility is still on the hunter to hit his target well for a clean kill. ➤

Photo by Bob Busby

These "mushroomed" bullets flanking the unfired bullet show the expansion potential of modern soft-point hunting ammunition. The larger diameter of the expanded slugs creates a larger wound channel and slows the bullet's passage through the target for a longer interval of energy release.

These x-ray photos show the effects of the expanding bullet and resulting energy release on a gelatin block. The photo sequence from top left to bottom right shows the bullet encountering the block, expanding and exiting. The wide channel behind the bullet and the "ballooning" effect are the result of energy release.

Photo courtesy of Winchester-Western

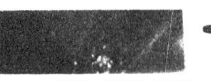

BEFORE ENTERING TARGET

3" PENETRATION OF TARGET

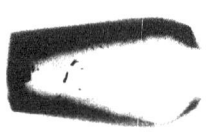

6" PENETRATION OF TARGET

CLEARING TARGET

Saltwater Sport

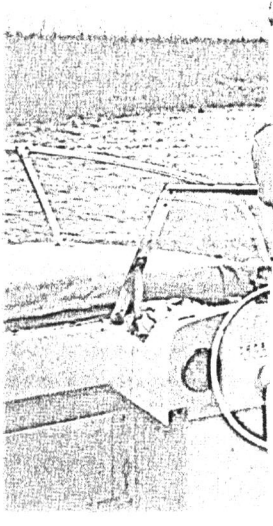

By T. Craig Martin

Photos by Jim Couch

Everyone knows Georgia has great freshwater fishing, but only about 5 percent of Georgia's fishermen sample our state's marvelous saltwater sport. The fishing is great along the coast now, and it just might be the time for you to try something new.

Inshore saltwater fishing technique isn't too complicated, but the search for speckled trout, channel bass, sheepshead, black drum and company is pretty complex, so you'd better have have a guide the first few times out. Hot spots along a saltwater shoreline don't much resemble their freshwater cousins, and the good holes, or "drops", vary with the tide.

A good guide can show you more in a day or two than you'll discover for yourself in months. Besides the good drops, a competent guide will point out sandbars waiting to trap you at low tide, recommend bait and tackle, and chart the quickest course to choice spots. He's not going to tell you everything he's learned in his years of saltwater fishing, but he'll give you a great start to fishing on your own.

Finding a good fishing spot may be the least of your worries in some of the coastal areas; newcomers can feel proud of themselves if they manage not to get lost or run aground. Most of the marinas are nestled along rivers that flow into the Atlantic; finding your way to the coast is easy, but threading your way among the

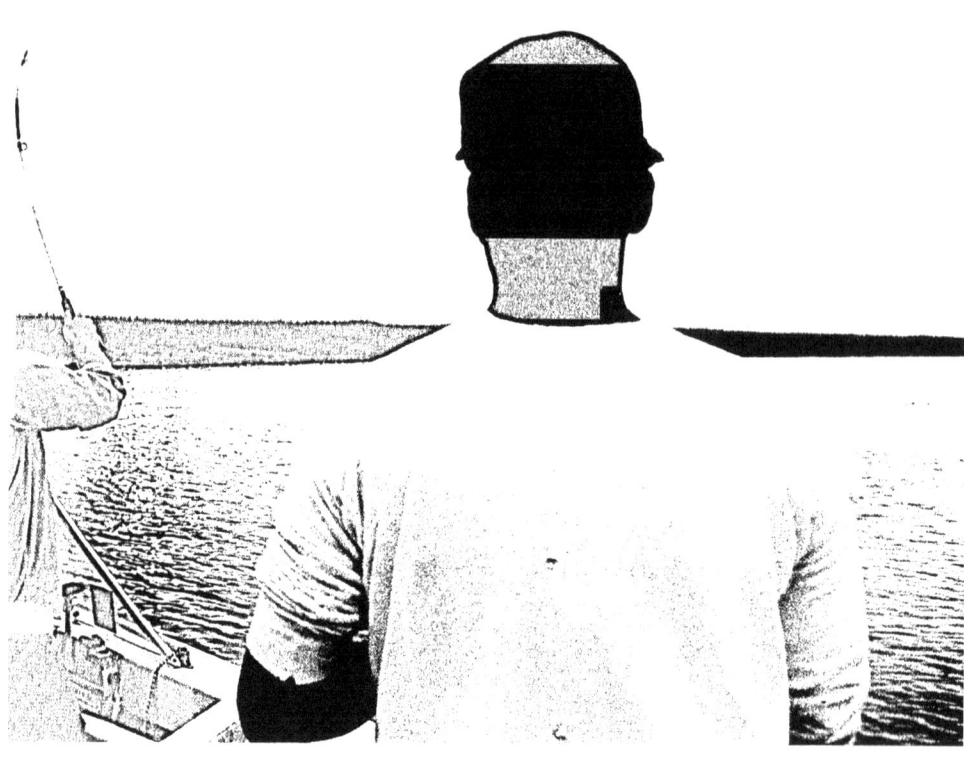

Bottom fishing with shrimp can lead to a cooler full of small black drum like this one. They're not tackle-busters, but are fun on light tackle and not bad eating.

pinched on above the bobber. Since you'll often be fishing at depths of 5 to 8 feet, there's a lot of line left out between the top weight and the bait when you cast, necessitating a two-hand, swinging cast. A long two-hand rod makes all this a lot easier. And while you won't need the extra backbone for most of the fish you catch (excluding that special 40-pound channel bass you luck onto), it will be helpful in throwing the heavy baits.

You'll often be fishing around oyster beds and shell-covered bottoms which can tear up dacron lines pretty fast, so mono seems the best choice. Any reel that will hold 200 or so yards of 15 or 20-pound line and has a good drag will put you in business. Some people recommend steel leaders and fancy shock tippets, but you can check with your guide or experienced locals before messing with them. Add to this a couple of the fluorescent saltwater bobbers, some weights, and 3/0 or 4/0 snelled hooks, and you're set for a great time.

Although shrimp are the most popular bait whenever they're available, other live or cut baits and many types of artificial lures take saltwater fish. Again, it's best to check with a guide or marina operator about baits popular in a particular area, but jigs, spoons, plugs, and streamer flies all produce. Recent reports suggest that leadhead plastic lures—called "Fuddlebug" by one manufacturer—are

very successful for trout and bass, perhaps because they resemble shrimp.

One other point on "equipment"—food. The stock at most of the marinas is somewhat less than elegant—perhaps less than palatable on rough days —and you might want to stock up on vittles before leaving home unless you thrive on vienna sausages (known along the coast as "vyannas") and saltines, washed down with pop and other suitable beverage.

Among the more popular fish along Georgia's coast are:

Speckled Trout: Known generally as "trout," this fellow really is a weakfish and is not related to the trout family at all. He does look a little like a trout, with his long slim shape and spotted back, but the two canine teeth at the tip of his upper jaw are enough to distinguish him immediately. Trout can be caught with almost any gear; but along the coast, the cork and shrimp method is preferred. The bait is cast out, and the cork jerked to cause a commotion on the surface; when the trout investigates, he finds the shrimp. He strikes at the head, so the shrimp should be hooked just behind the eyes. Keep alert: that bobber will dip under for just a second, and if you don't strike it'll be time to rebait.

Billy Prosser likes to fish for trout during an incoming tide, in clear water at the point of streams or creeks, and around oyster beds. Frank Culpepper

recommends ebb tides, but both agree that trout can be caught most anytime if you know the right drops. Shrimp are used until the first really cold spell, then plugs, spoons, and jigs take over. In all cases, the bait or lure should be kept moving in sharp jerks. And don't let the name weakfish fool you—trout aren't at all weak, and will put up a great fight on light tackle. They do have fairly soft mouths, however, so don't try to horse them in.

Where you catch one trout, you're apt to catch more, and hauls of 100 or more aren't unusual for a day's fishing.

Channel Bass: Known simply as "bass," which complicates things when you think you're asking questions about striped bass ... As you might have guessed, it's not even a bass, but really a member of the croaker family (as is the black drum which we'll discuss later). It's even called a "red drum," which may be more accurate, but hardly is descriptive, for the fish isn't really red. It has a copper or red shading, which makes it look reddish, but a better identifying mark is the black spot or spots at the base of the tail.

Bass can often be found in the same spots as trout, and you'll regularly see mixed stringers. But the bass seem to get around more, and surf fishermen take a lot of them casting just over the breakers with shrimp or plugs fished deep. Other anglers troll just beyond

8

A typical rig for speckled trout and channel bass: fluorescent bobber, swivel sinker, and snelled 4/0 or 5/0 hook. A shrimp hooked just behind the eyes is the most common bait.

the surf, or cast into it with plugs, spoons, jigs and streamer flies. These fish can be taken the year 'round, although late fall seems the best time for big bass. And a big bass is a pretty fair size fish, up to 30 or 40 pounds, although the inshore variety will run a bit smaller.

Unlike the trout, the bass will gently nudge live bait, and mouth it quite a bit before actually taking it—give him some time, then slam hard. He'll hit the artificials very hard, so there's no need to wait with them.

Black Drum: He's a bottom-feeder like the channel bass, but he prefers fairly quiet pools over sandy bottoms. He can be identified by the barbels, or whiskers, on his lower jaw and, in the younger fish, by black vertical stripes on his sides. Drum grow quite large, up to 150 pounds, and 30 pounders are not uncommon. Billy Prosser recently bested a 55 pounder after an hour fight off the dock of his marina. Almost any gear will do for drum fishing as long as it can get the dead shrimp or cut bait to the bottom. Small drum don't fight much, but the larger ones are great fun on light tackle. Since they usually cruise in schools, you often can fill your ice chest with drum once you find them.

Sheepshead: The small ones superficially resemble the black drum, but don't have the barbels and do have a much more impressive set of teeth. In fact, their unlikely mouth gives them

their name—it's rounded, and filled with flat grinding teeth, a few of which project at the front and look remarkably like a sheep's. Unlike the drum, sheepshead fight like the devil, although they're pretty small, only up to 4 pounds or so along our coast. They also are fine eating, which the drum usually aren't.

Sheepshead usually are found around bottom structures, feeding on small crustaceans. They are hard to catch, for they can snip off your bait without touching the hook, and do it so lightly you never notice. Be sure to use tough hooks when you fish for these guys, for they can bite right through light wire. They probably will frustrate you for a while, but once you get the touch you should do pretty well. Sheepshead aren't really a school fish, but they do seem to congregate in certain areas; if you get one, try again, there should be more around. And once you taste one, you'll want to search out more any time you can.

Striped Bass: Sometimes called "rockfish," this fish is increasingly popular in the freshwater lakes where it's been stocked by the Game and Fish Division of the Department of Natural Resources. But the saltwater version is great sport too, and even bigger than the freshwater variety, up to 70 or even 100 pounds. They can be found in bays and sounds now, and in the rivers during their spring spawning runs. The Ogeechee, Savan-

This 4-pound sheepshead put up a great fight against a medium-weight bottom fishing rig. Billy Prosser seemed to enjoy that fight as much as any in a day that ended with an ice chest full of trout, drum, and sheepshead.

nah, Altamaha, and St. Mary's rivers all are popular during these spring runs. At other times, surf rigs, heavy casting rods, and even fly rods are used successfully with a tremendous variety of lures.

Several other species are available to Georgia's inshore fishermen at various times of the year, including: Tarpon, American Shad, Southern Kingfish (whiting), and Flounder. They'll provide angling excitement if you'll search them out, and you may have more fun if you can get away from the traffic jams on the freshwater lakes.

The following marinas are listed in more or less north to south order by the nearest town. Most of them have someone around to give you information if you have the foresight to call ahead, and many can arrange guided trips if you give them enough warning.

We'll supply the marina name, manager's name, telephone number (all are area code 912), and nearest town. For specific information and directions, call the manager.

- Yellow Bluff Fishing Camp—Arthur Goodman—884-5448—Midway: Hoist, bait, tackle, cottages.
- Kip's Fishing Camp—Kip Smith—83-5162 —Townsend: Hoist, bait, tackle, boat rental, guides, restaurant, motel.
- Dasher's Marina—John Dasher—832-4992 —Townsend: Hoist, bait, tackle, guides, cottages, restaurant.
- Fisherman Lodge — George McNair — 832-4671—Darien: Hoist, ramp, bait, tackle, boat rental, guides, charter boat, motel, restaurant.
- McIntosh Rod & Gun Club—Italeen Stewart—437-4677—Darien: Ramp, hoist, bait.
- Two Way Fishing Camp—Frank Culpepper —265-9268—Darien: Hoist, bait, tackle, boat rental, guides, charter boat, camping.
- Troupe Creek Marina—Bob Gill—264-3862 —Brunswick: Hoist, bait, tackle, guides, snack bar.
- Crooked River State Park—Jerry Minchew —882-5256—Kingsland: Ramp, bait, camping.
- Savannah Marina—D. Wilson—897-1189— Thunderbolt: Launching ramp and hoist, bait, tackle, nearby restaurant.
- Chimney Creek Fishing Camp—L. L. Hogan —786-4751—Savannah Beach: Boat rental, hoist, bait, tackle, overnight camping.
- Tybee Marina—Dave Gomez—786-4996— Savannah Beach: Boat rental, launching ramp and hoist, bait, tackle, guides, nearby camping.
- Tuten's Fishing Camp & Marina — Henry Tuten — 355-9182 — Savannah: Boat rental, hoist, bait, tackle.
- Thunderbolt Marina—B. M. Hester—354-1260—Savannah: Hoist, bait, tackle, charter boat, restaurant.
- Kilkenny Fishing Camp — Robert Bacot — 756-3940—Richmond Hill: Ramp, hoist, bait, tackle, camping.
- Branch's Marina—Bill Prosser—884-5819— Midway: Hoist, bait, tackle, boat rental, guide, charter boat, camping, cottage.
- Hoke Youman's Fishing Camp—Hoke Youman—884-5449—Midway; Charter boat.

This Tide Table for 1973 is furnished to you compliments of OUTDOORS IN GEORGIA for your use in coastal fishing and hunting.

Fold it and put it in your tackle box, hunting coat, or wherever it will always be handy, for use all year long.

To keep up to date on everything about outdoor recreation in Georgia, keep up your OUTDOORS IN GEORGIA subscription. For new subscriptions, send $3.00 for a year or $5.00 for two years to OUTDOORS IN GEORGIA, 270 Washington St., S.W., Atlanta, Georgia 30334. For renewals, please furnish the address label off your latest issue.

P.S. Please remember . . . be a good sportsman. Obey all Game and Fish regulations, and don't litter!

1973 GEORGIA TIDE TABLES

Times given are Eastern Standard—adjust for Daylight Saving by adding one hour.

Calculations are for Savannah River Entrance. Corrections for other locations can be made by using the accompanying tidal difference data. Merely add or subtract the correction as indicated for the specific location.

		DIFFERENCES Time	
GEORGIA		High Water	Low Water
	Savannah River		
2707	Tybee Light	−0 08	−0 15
2715	Port Wentworth	+0 33	+0 41
	Tybee Creek and Wassaw Sound		
2719	Tybee Creek entrance . . .	−0 07	+0 02
2727	Thunderbolt	+0 34	+0 09
2731	Isle of Hope, Skidaway River	+0 52	+0 25
	Ossabaw Sound		
2733	Egg Islands	+0 06	+0 07
2739	Fort McAllister, Ogeechee R.	+0 50	+1 13
2743	Cane Patch Creek entrance .	+0 57	+0 40
	St. Catherines and Sapelo Sounds		
2747	Kilkenny Club, Kilkenny Cr. .	+0 31	+0 13
2749	Sunbury, Medway River . .	+0 56	+0 42
2757	Blackbeard Island	+0 20	+0 19
2761	Mud R., at Old Teakettle Cr.	+0 47	+0 43

		DIFFERENCES Time	
	Doboy and Altamaha	High Water	Low Water
	Sounds		
2762	Blackbeard Cr., Blackbeard I.	+0 21	+0 44
2763	Sapelo Island	0 00	+0 02
2769	Darien, Darien River. . . .	+1 10	+1 12
2771	Wolf Island	+0 06	+0 35
2773	Champney I., S. Altamaha R.	+1 12	+2 30
	St. Simons Sound		
2779	St. Simons Sound bar . . .	+0 01	−0 05
2781	St. Simons Light	+0 24	+0 28
2785	Troup Cr. entr., Mackay R. .	+0 54	+0 49
2787	Brunswick, East River . . .	+0 55	+0 40
	St. Andrew Sound		
2797	Jekyll Point	+0 28	+0 28
2799	Jointer Island, Jointer Creek	+1 02	+0 49
2807	Dover Bluff, Dover Creek . .	+0 57	+0 49
2817	Cumberland Wh., Cumb. R. .	+0 40	+0 42
	Cumberland Sound		
2821	St. Marys Entr., north jetty .	+0 15	+0 15
2823	Crooked River entrance . .	+1 23	+1 12
2825	Harrietts Bluff, Crooked River	+2 09	+2 12
2827	St. Marys, St. Marys River. .	+1 21	+1 13

JANUARY, 1973

Day	A.M.	High Water Ht.	P.M.	Ht.	Low Water A.M.	P.M.
1 Mon.	5:51	6.7	5:51	5.7	11:57	11:59
2 Tue.	6:32	6.8	6:33	5.8	—	12:43
3 Wed.	7:11	7.0	7:11	6.0	12:42	1:26
4 Thu.	7:45	7.1	7:50	6.1	1:27	2:09
5 Fri.	8:18	7.1	8:25	6.2	2:09	2:47
6 Sat.	8:51	7.0	9:01	6.3	2:46	3:25
7 Sun.	9:27	7.0	9:42	6.4	3:27	4:03
8 Mon.	10:07	6.8	10:25	6.5	4:05	4:42
9 Tue.	10:48	6.6	11:14	6.6	4:48	5:19
10 Wed.	11:34	6.4	—		5:33	6:08
11 Thu.	12:07	6.7	12:27	6.2	6:32	7:00
12 Fri.	1:04	6.8	1:24	6.0	7:35	8:03
13 Sat.	2:06	6.9	2:27	5.9	8:45	9:06
14 Sun.	3:15	7.0	3:41	5.8	9:54	10:11
15 Mon.	4:27	7.3	4:55	6.0	10:56	11:11
16 Tue.	5:35	7.6	6:00	6.4	11:57	—
17 Wed.	6:33	7.9	6:58	6.7	12:10	12:55
18 Thu.	7:27	8.1	7:53	7.0	1:08	1:48
19 Fri.	8:16	8.2	8:42	7.2	2:02	2:37
20 Sat.	9:02	8.0	9:27	7.1	2:53	3:26
21 Sun.	9:48	7.6	10:18	7.0	3:42	4:09
22 Mon.	10:34	7.2	11:04	6.8	4:29	4:51
23 Tue.	11:17	6.7	11:53	6.6	5:16	5:34
24 Wed.	11:58	6.2	—		6:01	6:17
25 Thu.	12:38	6.3	12:44	5.8	6:53	7:06
26 Fri.	1:27	6.1	1:31	5.5	7:46	8:01
27 Sat.	2:18	5.9	2:23	5.3	8:45	8:55
28 Sun.	3:15	5.9	3:20	5.2	9:41	9:48
29 Mon.	4:17	5.9	4:18	5.2	10:36	10:40
30 Tue.	5:12	6.2	5:19	5.4	11:25	11:30
31 Wed.	6:03	6.4	6:07	5:6	—	12:13

Moon Phases:
New Moon 4th, 1st Qtr. 12th, Full Moon 18th, Last Qtr. 26th

FEBRUARY, 1973

Day	A.M.	High Water Ht.	P.M.	Ht.	Low Water A.M.	P.M.
1 Thu.	6:45	6.7	6:48	5.9	12:16	12:59
2 Fri.	7:21	6.9	7:28	6.2	1:02	1:40
3 Sat.	7:56	7.0	8:04	6.5	1:45	2:21
4 Sun.	8:32	7.1	8:42	6.7	2:26	2:58
5 Mon.	9:06	7.0	9:21	6.9	3:07	3:34
6 Tue.	9:43	6.9	10:04	7.1	3:48	4:12
7 Wed.	10:26	6.7	10:53	7.1	4:31	4:55
8 Thu.	11:13	6.4	11:45	7.0	5:16	5:40
9 Fri.	—		12:06	6.1	6:12	6:35
10 Sat.	12:44	6.9	1:03	5.8	7:15	7:38
11 Sun.	1:47	6.8	2:13	5.6	8:26	8:48
12 Mon.	2:59	6.8	3:29	5.6	9:39	9:55
13 Tue.	4:13	6.9	4:49	5.9	10:43	10:59
14 Wed.	5:24	7.2	5:54	6.4	11:43	11:59
15 Thu.	6:24	7.6	6:51	6.9	—	12:38
16 Fri.	7:13	7.8	7:40	7.2	12:54	1:30
17 Sat.	8:00	7.8	8:25	7.4	1:45	2:15
18 Sun.	8:41	7.6	9:07	7.4	2:34	2:58
19 Mon.	9:21	7.4	9:48	7.3	3:21	3:38
20 Tue.	10:02	7.0	10:28	7.0	4:03	4:16
21 Wed.	10:38	6.6	11:07	6.7	4:44	4:54
22 Thu.	11:16	6.1	11:49	6.4	5:26	5:35
23 Fri.	11:58	5.8	—		6:11	6:18
24 Sat.	12:35	6.1	12:43	5.5	7:02	7:10
25 Sun.	1:26	5.9	1:34	5.3	7:59	8:07
26 Mon.	2:20	5.8	2:31	5.2	9:00	9:07
27 Tue.	3:23	5.8	3:34	5.2	9:57	10:05
28 Wed.	4:29	6.0	4:37	5.5	10:50	10:59

Moon Phases:
New Moon 3rd, 1st Qtr. 10th, Full Moon 17th, Last Qtr. 25th

MARCH, 1973

Day	A.M.	High Water Ht.	P.M.	Ht.	Low Water A.M.	P.M.
1 Thu.	5:24	6.3	5:33	5.9	11:39	11:47
2 Fri.	6:10	6.6	6:20	6.3	—	12:23
3 Sat.	6:49	6.9	7:01	6.8	12:33	1:06
4 Sun.	7:30	7.1	7:40	7.2	1:21	1:47
5 Mon.	8:06	7.2	8:21	7.5	2:05	2:28
6 Tue.	8:42	7.1	9:01	7.7	2:46	3:08
7 Wed.	9:22	7.0	9:46	7.7	3:29	3:47
8 Thu.	10:09	6.8	10:35	7.6	4:15	4:32
9 Fri.	10:56	6.5	11:30	7.4	5:04	5:21
10 Sat.	11:52	6.1	—		5:59	6:17
11 Sun.	12:27	7.1	12:57	5.9	7:02	9:24
12 Mon.	1:35	6.9	2:08	5.9	8:14	8:36
13 Tue.	2:48	6.8	3:27	5.8	9:26	9:46
14 Wed.	4:01	6.8	4:42	6.2	10:29	10:49
15 Thu.	5:12	7.1	5:47	6.7	11:25	11:48
16 Fri.	6:07	7.3	6:35	7.2	—	12:16
17 Sat.	6:55	7.5	7:24	7.6	12:39	1:04
18 Sun.	7:37	7.5	8:01	7.7	1:29	1:48
19 Mon.	8:14	7.3	8:40	7.7	2:14	2:28
20 Tue.	8:52	7.1	9:15	7.5	2:57	3:06
21 Wed.	9:26	6.8	9:51	7.3	3:37	3:42
22 Thu.	10:01	6.5	10:28	7.0	4:15	4:19
23 Fri.	10:38	6.1	11:07	6.8	4:54	4:57
24 Sat.	11:17	5.9	11:48	6.3	5:36	5:36
25 Sun.	—		12:06	5.6	6:21	6:25
26 Mon.	12:38	6.1	12:53	5.5	7:17	7:22
27 Tue.	1:31	5.9	1:50	5.4	8:16	8:25
28 Wed.	2:32	5.9	2:54	5.5	9:16	9:28
29 Thu.	3:35	6.0	3:55	5.8	10:11	10:27
30 Fri.	4:36	6.3	4:53	6.3	10:58	11:15
31 Sat.	5:27	6.6	5:47	6.9	11:46	—

Moon Phases:
New Moon 5th, 1st Qtr. 11th, Full Moon 18th, Last Qtr. 26th

APRIL, 1973

Day	A.M.	High Water Ht.	P.M.	Ht.	Low Water A.M.	P.M.
1 Sun.	6:15	6.9	6:31	7.4	12:04	12:29
2 Mon.	6:56	7.1	7:14	7.9	12:52	1:13
3 Tue.	7:39	7.2	7:57	8.3	1:40	1:56
4 Wed.	8:20	7.2	8:42	8.4	2:26	2:41
5 Thu.	9:04	7.1	9:27	8.3	3:15	3:26
6 Fri.	9:53	6.8	10:20	8.1	4:02	4:14
7 Sat.	10:48	6.5	11:16	7.7	4:54	5:07
8 Sun.	11:49	6.3	—		5:49	6:06
9 Mon.	12:19	7.3	12:56	6.1	6:53	7:15
10 Tue.	1:25	7.0	2:07	6.1	8:02	8:26
11 Wed.	2:35	6.8	3:22	6.3	9:08	9:33
12 Thu.	3:46	6.8	4:30	6.7	10:07	10:34
13 Fri.	4:49	6.9	5:27	7.1	11:02	11:28
14 Sat.	5:44	7.0	6:16	7.5	11:49	—
15 Sun.	6:32	7.0	6:59	7.8	12:19	12:34
16 Mon.	7:11	7.0	7:36	7.8	1:06	1:17
17 Tue.	7:46	6.9	8:13	7.8	1:49	1:55
18 Wed.	8:21	6.7	8:45	7.6	2:32	2:35
19 Thu.	8:55	6.5	9:20	7.4	3:11	3:11
20 Fri.	9:28	6.3	9:54	7.1	3:50	3:47
21 Sat.	10:03	6.1	10:31	6.8	4:25	4:22
22 Sun.	10:46	5.9	11:14	6.6	5:08	5:03
23 Mon.	11:29	5.7	—		5:51	5:46
24 Tue.	12:01	6.4	12:21	5.7	6:40	6:43
25 Wed.	12:50	6.2	1:16	5.7	7:35	7:43
26 Thu.	1:44	6.1	2:15	5.9	8:31	8:47
27 Fri.	2:43	6.1	3:14	6.3	9:26	9:48
28 Sat.	3:42	6.3	4:14	6.8	10:16	10:42
29 Sun.	4:43	6.5	5:09	7.4	11:05	11:35
30 Mon.	5:36	6.7	6:00	7.9	11:51	—

Moon Phases:
New Moon 3rd, 1st Qtr. 10th, Full Moon 17th, Last Qtr. 25th

MAY, 1973

Day	A.M.	Ht.	P.M.	Ht.	A.M.	P.M.
	High Water				Low Water	
1 Tue.	6:25	6.9	6:48	8.4	12:26	12:39
2 Wed.	7:13	7.1	7:36	8.7	1:17	1:28
3 Thu.	8:02	7.1	8:26	8.7	2:08	2:17
4 Fri.	8:49	7.0	9:15	8.6	2:59	3:09
5 Sat.	9:42	6.9	10:10	8.3	3:50	4:01
6 Sun.	10:41	6.6	10:07	7.9	4:44	4:56
7 Mon.	11:45	6.5	—	—	5:39	5:55
8 Tue.	12:10	7.5	12:51	6.4	6:40	7:00
9 Wed.	1:13	7.1	2:01	6.5	7:42	8:09
10 Thu.	2:16	6.8	3:04	6.6	8:43	9:15
11 Fri.	3:19	6.6	4:05	6.9	9:40	10:14
12 Sat.	4:19	6.5	5:04	7.2	10:29	11:05
13 Sun.	5:12	6.5	5:50	7.5	11:15	11:54
14 Mon.	5:57	6.5	6:33	7.6	—	12:01
15 Tue.	6:42	6.5	7:12	7.7	12:39	12:45
16 Wed.	7:19	6.4	7:45	7.6	1:23	1:24
17 Thu.	7:52	6.3	8:20	7.5	2:06	2:04
18 Fri.	8:26	6.2	8:52	7.3	2:45	2:42
19 Sat.	9:01	6.1	9:27	7.1	3:25	3:19
20 Sun.	9:37	6.0	10:02	6.9	4:03	3:57
21 Mon.	10:18	5.9	10:41	6.7	4:41	4:36
22 Tue.	11:03	5.9	11:26	6.5	5:22	5:18
23 Wed.	11:52	5.9	—	—	6:05	6:08
24 Thu.	12:14	6.4	12:45	6.1	6:53	7:04
25 Fri.	1:03	6.3	1:38	6.3	7:45	8:07
26 Sat.	1:56	6.2	2:34	6.7	8:41	9:11
27 Sun.	2:55	6.2	3:33	7.1	9:34	10:08
28 Mon.	3:56	6.3	4:34	7.6	10:20	11:06
29 Tue.	4:59	6.5	5:31	8.1	11:17	—
30 Wed.	5:57	6.7	6:29	8.5	12:01	12:10
31 Thu.	6:52	6.9	7:18	8.7	12:56	1:04

Moon Phases:
New Moon 2nd, 1st Qtr. 9th, Full Moon 17th, Last Qtr. 25th

JUNE, 1973

Day	A.M.	Ht.	P.M.	Ht.	A.M.	P.M.
	High Water				Low Water	
1 Fri.	7:45	7.0	8:11	8.8	1:50	2:00
2 Sat.	8:39	7.0	9:04	8.6	2:45	2:54
3 Sun.	9:34	6.9	9:59	8.3	3:38	3:49
4 Mon.	10:35	6.8	10:54	7.9	4:31	4:44
5 Tue.	11:36	6.8	11:52	7.5	5:23	5:40
6 Wed.	12:37	6.7	—	—	6:17	6:43
7 Thu.	12:50	7.1	1:36	6.7	7:15	7:45
8 Fri.	1:45	6.7	2:35	6.8	8:10	8:46
9 Sat.	2:41	6.3	3:35	6.9	9:04	9:45
10 Sun.	3:36	6.1	4:30	7.0	9:55	10:39
11 Mon.	4:37	6.0	5:19	7.1	10:42	11:24
12 Tue.	5:24	5.9	6:04	7.3	11:27	—
13 Wed.	6:10	6.0	6:45	7.3	12:13	12:12
14 Thu.	6:51	6.0	7:22	7.4	12:56	12:55
15 Fri.	7:26	6.0	7:57	7.3	1:41	1:36
16 Sat.	8:03	6.0	8:29	7.3	2:22	2:16
17 Sun.	8:39	6.0	9:04	7.1	3:01	2:56
18 Mon.	9:14	6.0	9:38	7.0	3:40	3:35
19 Tue.	9:53	6.0	10:15	6.8	4:17	4:12
20 Wed.	10:38	6.1	10:54	6.7	4:54	4:53
21 Thu.	11:23	6.3	11:39	6.5	5:33	5:36
22 Fri.	—	—	12:11	6.5	6:17	6:33
23 Sat.	12:26	6.4	1:06	6.7	7:03	7:31
24 Sun.	1:19	6.3	2:01	7.0	8:00	8:38
25 Mon.	2:17	6.1	3:02	7.3	8:58	9:39
26 Tue.	3:20	6.1	4:06	7.6	9:55	10:40
27 Wed.	4:27	6.2	5:09	8.0	10:53	11:41
28 Thu.	5:35	6.4	6:10	8.4	11:49	—
29 Fri.	6:36	6.7	7:07	8.6	12:39	12:49
30 Sat.	7:41	7.0	7:59	8.7	1:37	1:46

Moon Phases:
New Moon 1st and 30th, 1st Qtr. 7th, Full Moon 15th, Last Qtr. 23rd

JULY, 1973

Day	A.M.	Ht.	P.M.	Ht.	A.M.	P.M.
	High Water				Low Water	
1 Sun.	8:27	7.1	8:53	8.6	2:31	2:41
2 Mon.	9:24	7.2	9:44	8.3	3:22	3:35
3 Tue.	10:19	7.2	10:36	7.9	4:11	4:28
4 Wed.	11:16	7.1	11:28	7.4	5:00	5:22
5 Thu.	12:11	7.0	—	—	5:49	6:15
6 Fri.	12:17	6.9	1:05	6.9	6:40	7:14
7 Sat.	1:09	6.5	1:59	6.8	7:32	8:13
8 Sun.	2:01	6.1	2:52	6.7	8:25	9:09
9 Mon.	2:55	5.8	3:51	6.7	9:16	10:04
10 Tue.	3:48	5.6	4:44	6.8	10:07	10:53
11 Wed.	4:44	5.6	5:35	6.9	10:56	11:44
12 Thu.	5:35	5.7	6:19	7.1	11:41	—
13 Fri.	6:22	5.8	6:58	7.2	12:29	12:26
14 Sat.	7:03	6.0	7:34	7.3	1:13	1:10
15 Sun.	7:40	6.1	8:08	7.3	1:56	1:53
16 Mon.	8:18	6.3	8:41	7.3	2:37	2:34
17 Tue.	8:51	6.4	9:13	7.2	3:13	3:12
18 Wed.	9:31	6.5	9:50	7.0	3:49	3:51
19 Thu.	10:10	6.7	10:25	6.9	4:25	4:28
20 Fri.	10:54	6.8	11:08	6.7	5:00	5:14
21 Sat.	11:42	7.0	11:55	6.5	5:43	6:03
22 Sun.	—	—	12:37	7.1	6:30	7:02
23 Mon.	12:49	6.3	1:34	7.2	7:26	8:09
24 Tue.	1:48	6.1	2:36	7.4	8:29	9:18
25 Wed.	2:55	6.0	3:45	7.6	9:32	10:23
26 Thu.	4:11	6.1	4:56	7.9	10:34	11:25
27 Fri.	5:22	6.4	5:59	8.2	11:35	—
28 Sat.	6:26	6.9	6:56	8.5	12:23	12:35
29 Sun.	7:24	7.3	7:47	8.7	1:19	1:32
30 Mon.	8:17	7.5	8:36	8.6	2:12	2:26
31 Tue.	9:08	7.7	9:22	8.3	3:01	3:17

Moon Phases:
1st Qtr. 7th, Full Moon 15th, Last Qtr. 23rd, New Moon 29th

AUGUST, 1973

Day	A.M.	Ht.	P.M.	Ht.	A.M.	P.M.
	High Water				Low Water	
1 Wed.	9:56	7.7	10:11	7.9	3:46	4:09
2 Thu.	10:46	7.5	10:54	7.4	4:32	4:55
3 Fri.	11:37	7.3	11:43	6.9	5:16	5:44
4 Sat.	—	—	12:25	7.1	6:02	6:37
5 Sun.	12:29	6.4	1:15	6.8	6:50	7:31
6 Mon.	1:15	6.0	2:09	6.6	7:41	8:30
7 Tue.	2:08	5.7	3:04	6.5	8:35	9:27
8 Wed.	3:04	5.6	4:04	6.6	9:31	10:20
9 Thu.	4:05	5.6	4:59	6.7	10:24	11:14
10 Fri.	5:02	5.8	5:48	7.0	11:14	11:59
11 Sat.	5:53	6.0	6:29	7.2	—	12:01
12 Sun.	6:37	6.3	7:08	7.4	12:42	12:45
13 Mon.	7:16	6.6	7:41	7.5	1:27	1:27
14 Tue.	7:52	6.9	8:15	7.5	2:06	2:09
15 Wed.	8:27	7.1	8:48	7.5	2:41	2:48
16 Thu.	9:06	7.3	9:22	7.3	3:17	3:27
17 Fri.	9:43	7.5	9:59	7.1	3:54	4:08
18 Sat.	10:28	7.5	10:42	6.9	4:32	4:51
19 Sun.	11:17	7.5	11:31	6.7	5:13	5:42
20 Mon.	—	—	12:11	7.5	6:02	6:40
21 Tue.	12:28	6.4	1:12	7.5	6:59	7:49
22 Wed.	1:31	6.2	2:19	7.5	8:08	9:02
23 Thu.	2:45	6.1	3:33	7.6	9:18	10:11
24 Fri.	4:04	6.3	4:43	7.8	10:24	11:12
25 Sat.	5:15	6.8	5:48	8.2	11:25	—
26 Sun.	6:18	7.3	6:43	8.5	12:07	12:23
27 Mon.	7:11	7.8	7:33	8.6	1:00	1:18
28 Tue.	8:00	8.1	8:16	8.5	1:49	2:09
29 Wed.	8:45	8.2	8:57	8.2	2:35	2:58
30 Thu.	9:29	8.1	9:40	7.8	3:18	3:43
31 Fri.	10:15	7.9	10:20	7.4	3:59	4:27

Moon Phases:
1st Qtr. 5th, Full Moon 14th, Last Qtr. 21st, New Moon 28th

SEPTEMBER, 1973

Day	A.M.	High Water Ht.	P.M.	Ht.	Low Water A.M.	P.M.
1 Sat.	10:57	7.6	11:01	6.9	4:39	5:13
2 Sun.	11:42	7.2	11:45	6.5	5:20	5:58
3 Mon.	—	—	12:30	6.9	6:06	6:50
4 Tue.	12:30	6.1	1:21	6.7	6:56	7:47
5 Wed.	1:25	5.9	2:16	6.5	7:53	8:49
6 Thu.	2:20	5.8	3:16	6.6	8:53	9:48
7 Fri.	3:23	5.8	4:18	6.7	9:49	10:37
8 Sat.	4:24	6.0	5:09	7.0	10:42	11:24
9 Sun.	5:19	6.4	5:57	7.3	11:31	—
10 Mon.	6:04	6.8	6:36	7.5	12:07	12:16
11 Tue.	6:45	7.3	7:13	7.7	12:48	1:01
12 Wed.	7:23	7.7	7:45	7.7	1:27	1:42
13 Thu.	7:59	8.0	8:19	7.7	2:07	2:25
14 Fri.	8:39	8.2	8:57	7.6	2:45	3:06
15 Sat.	9:21	8.2	9:36	7.4	3:24	3:49
16 Sun.	10:04	8.2	10:23	7.1	4:07	4:35
17 Mon.	10:57	8.0	11:14	6.8	4:51	5:26
18 Tue.	11:56	7.8	—	—	5:45	6:27
19 Wed.	12:18	6.5	12:59	7.6	6:47	7:38
20 Thu.	1:25	6.4	2:09	7.5	7:58	8:51
21 Fri.	2:44	6.4	3:23	7.6	9:10	9:56
22 Sat.	4:01	6.8	4:34	7.8	10:16	10:55
23 Sun.	5:10	7.3	5:34	8.1	11:15	11:47
24 Mon.	6:07	7.8	6:25	8.3	—	12:10
25 Tue.	6:55	8.3	7:11	8.3	12:36	1:01
26 Wed.	7:40	8.5	7:51	8.2	1:23	1:49
27 Thu.	8:19	8.5	8:32	8.0	2:06	2:36
28 Fri.	9:00	8.4	9:08	7.6	2:46	3:19
29 Sat.	9:39	8.1	9:46	7.2	3:27	4:00
30 Sun.	10:17	7.7	10:25	6.8	4:06	4:41

Moon Phases:
1st Qtr. 4th, Full Moon 12th, Last Qtr. 19th, New Moon 26th

OCTOBER, 1973

Day	A.M.	High Water Ht.	P.M.	Ht.	Low Water A.M.	P.M.
1 Mon.	11:00	7.4	11:04	6.5	4:44	5:23
2 Tue.	11:45	7.0	11:53	6.2	5:27	6:11
3 Wed.	—	—	12:35	6.8	6:14	7:04
4 Thu.	12:44	6.0	1:28	6.6	7:09	8:05
5 Fri.	1:41	6.0	2:24	6.6	8:12	9:05
6 Sat.	2:39	6.1	3:26	6.7	9:14	9:56
7 Sun.	3:42	6.3	4:21	6.9	10:07	10:43
8 Mon.	4:38	6.8	5:12	7.2	10:58	11:28
9 Tue.	5:27	7.3	5:55	7.4	11:48	—
10 Wed.	6:13	7.8	6:36	7.6	12:10	12:32
11 Thu.	6:55	8.3	7:16	7.7	12:52	1:17
12 Fri.	7:34	8.6	7:53	7.7	1:34	2:02
13 Sat.	8:17	8.8	8:34	7.6	2:17	2:48
14 Sun.	9:02	8.8	9:20	7.4	3:01	3:34
15 Mon.	9:51	8.6	10:11	7.1	3:46	4:22
16 Tue.	10:44	8.3	11:08	6.8	4:36	5:17
17 Wed.	11:45	8.0	—	—	5:33	6:17
18 Thu.	12:15	6.6	12:51	7.7	6:36	7:25
19 Fri.	1:25	6.6	2:01	7.5	7:47	8:35
20 Sat.	2:39	6.7	3:07	7.5	9:00	9:38
21 Sun.	3:52	7.1	4:16	7.5	10:03	10:33
22 Mon.	4:56	7.6	5:15	7.6	10:58	11:22
23 Tue.	5:51	8.0	6:04	7.7	11:52	—
24 Wed.	6:36	8.3	6:48	7.7	12:10	12:41
25 Thu.	7:17	8.5	7:29	7.6	12:54	1:27
26 Fri.	7:56	8.4	8:03	7.4	1:37	2:12
27 Sat.	8:32	8.3	8:39	7.2	2:18	2:53
28 Sun.	9:10	8.0	9:15	6.9	2:56	3:33
29 Mon.	9:43	7.7	9:52	6.6	3:34	4:12
30 Tue.	10:22	7.3	10:31	6.4	4:13	4:54
31 Wed.	11:05	7.0	11:16	6.2	4:54	5:36

Moon Phases:
1st Qtr. 4th, Full Moon 12th, Last Qtr. 18th, New Moon 26th

NOVEMBER, 1973

Day	A.M.	High Water Ht.	P.M.	Ht.	Low Water A.M.	P.M.
1 Thu.	11:52	6.8	—	—	5:37	6:27
2 Fri.	12:05	6.1	12:43	6.6	6:30	7:20
3 Sat.	12:59	6.1	1:34	6.5	7:28	8:16
4 Sun.	2:00	6.2	2:30	6.5	8:29	9:10
5 Mon.	2:55	6.5	3:27	6.6	9:28	10:01
6 Tue.	3:52	6.9	4:20	6.8	10:21	10:46
7 Wed.	4:48	7.4	5:13	7.0	11:12	11:30
8 Thu.	5:37	8.0	6:02	7.2	—	12:03
9 Fri.	6:25	8.4	6:46	7.4	12:16	12:51
10 Sat.	7:11	8.8	7:33	7.4	1:04	1:40
11 Sun.	8:00	8.9	8:20	7.4	1:52	2:29
12 Mon.	8:48	8.9	9:09	7.3	2:41	3:21
13 Tue.	9:39	8.6	10:04	7.1	3:32	4:12
14 Wed.	10:36	8.3	11:04	6.8	4:25	5:07
15 Thu.	11:33	7.9	—	—	5:23	6:05
16 Fri.	12:11	6.7	12:37	7.6	6:24	7:06
17 Sat.	1:19	6.7	1:41	7.3	7:34	8:10
18 Sun.	2:27	6.9	2:46	7.0	8:41	9:13
19 Mon.	3:36	7.1	3:49	6.9	9:45	10:04
20 Tue.	4:33	7.4	4:45	6.9	10:40	10:55
21 Wed.	5:28	7.7	5:38	6.9	11:31	11:41
22 Thu.	6:14	7.9	6:23	6.9	—	12:20
23 Fri.	6:57	8.0	7:02	6.8	12:26	1:05
24 Sat.	7:34	7.9	7:40	6.8	1:09	1:47
25 Sun.	8:10	7.8	8:14	6.6	1:50	2:29
26 Mon.	8:44	7.6	8:50	6.5	2:30	3:11
27 Tue.	9:18	7.4	9:25	6.3	3:09	3:50
28 Wed.	9:53	7.1	10:03	6.2	3:46	4:28
29 Thu.	10:32	6.9	10:48	6.1	4:25	5:07
30 Fri.	11:13	6.7	11:33	6.1	5:07	5:55

Moon Phases:
1st Qtr. 3rd, Full Moon 10th, Last Qtr. 17th, New Moon 24th

DECEMBER, 1973

Day	A.M.	High Water Ht.	P.M.	Ht.	Low Water A.M.	P.M.
1 Sat.	11:58	6.5	—	—	5:50	6:34
2 Sun.	12:22	6.1	12:48	6.4	6:43	7:27
3 Mon.	1:15	6.3	1:39	6.3	7:43	8:20
4 Tue.	2:12	6.5	2:32	6.2	8:45	9:13
5 Wed.	3:06	6.9	3:31	6.3	9:45	10:05
6 Thu.	4:07	7.3	4:30	6.4	10:40	10:55
7 Fri.	5:08	7.7	5:28	6.6	11:35	11:47
8 Sat.	6:03	8.2	6:23	6.9	—	12:28
9 Sun.	6:55	8.5	7:16	7.0	12:39	1:21
10 Mon.	7:46	8.7	8:07	7.1	1:33	2:15
11 Tue.	8:37	8.7	9:01	7.1	2:26	3:09
12 Wed.	9:30	8.5	9:57	7.1	3:21	4:00
13 Thu.	10:25	8.1	10:57	6.9	4:15	4:52
14 Fri.	11:20	7.7	11:58	6.9	5:10	5:45
15 Sat.	—	—	12:17	7.3	6:09	6:40
16 Sun.	12:59	6.8	1:16	6.8	7:12	7:41
17 Mon.	2:02	6.8	2:15	6.5	8:17	8:39
18 Tue.	3:03	6.8	3:11	6.2	9:18	9:34
19 Wed.	4:05	6.9	4:12	6.0	10:13	10:27
20 Thu.	5:02	7.0	5:09	6.0	11:05	11:12
21 Fri.	5:51	7.1	5:54	6.0	11:54	11:59
22 Sat.	6:36	7.2	6:38	6.1	—	12:39
23 Sun.	7:13	7.3	7:17	6.1	12:44	1:24
24 Mon.	7:50	7.3	7:54	6.2	1:27	2:07
25 Tue.	8:25	7.2	8:29	6.2	2:08	2:48
26 Wed.	8:57	7.1	9:01	6.1	2:45	3:25
27 Thu.	9:30	6.9	9:38	6.1	3:24	4:02
28 Fri.	10:04	6.7	10:19	6.1	3:59	4:38
29 Sat.	10:39	6.6	11:00	6.2	4:38	5:14
30 Sun.	11:20	6.4	11:45	6.3	5:19	5:55
31 Mon.	—	—	12:03	6.2	6:06	6:38

Moon Phases:
1st Qtr. 3rd, Full Moon 10th, Last Qtr. 16th, New Moon 24th

BIG DEER CONTEST

By Aaron Pass

Georgia deer hunters who hope to compete in the upcoming Big Deer Contest for deer killed in the 1972-73 hunting season will have to "Rack-up" to enter their trophy. Future judging of all entries for prizes and awards will be done on the basis of **rack size only**, and deer weight will no longer be considered as a category. The contest, which is jointly sponsored by the Georgia Sportsman's Federation and **Outdoors in Georgia**, the magazine of the Department of Natural Resources, has become an annual event. It has formerly listed categories for Typical Rack, Non-typical Rack, and Weight. The elimination of the weight category was one of several changes made in this year's contest.

Charles Ingram, President of the Georgia Sportsman's Federation, and Jack Crockford, Director of the Game and Fish Division of the Department of Natural Resources met this past summer to revise the contest rules and categories. The changes made are intended to sim-plify the judging of the contest and reduce the chance of "accidental inequities." According to Crockford, "The restriction of the judging to antler size only more realis-tically represents the ideal of the 'Trophy Hunter.' It also provides precise measurements taken under a proven measuring system which can be compared again and again, if necessary, to determine the winner."

All racks will be measured by competent wildlife biologists of the Game and Fish Division using the Boone and Crockett system of measurement. Any hunter who kills a buck with an out-size rack should take it to the nearest Game Management Regional Field Office for measurement after the antlers have air-dried for 60 days. Typical racks scoring more than 150 points under the Boone and Crockett system of measurement or non-typical racks scoring 175 or more points are eligible for entry in the contest. Note that the Boone and Crock-ett system allows for the measurement of all dimensions

15

of the rack and converts these dimensions to a point scale. It **Does not** refer to the number of antler points or projections on the rack.

Winners of the contest will be hosted by the Georgia Sportsman's Federation at the Federation's annual banquet where they will be awarded prizes as part of the awards program. Each entrant in the contest will receive from the Department of Natural Resources a Master Hunter Certificate noting the hunter's name, date and place of kill and final score of antlers.

The following is an updated listing of the rules for the Big Deer Contest which apply to the 1972-73 contest. Immediately below the list of rules is listed the official measuring stations of the contest. It is advised that all entrants should call for an appointment to measure their trophies.

1971 CONTEST WINNERS

TYPICAL RACK
H. D. Cannon of Comer, Ga.—170 2/8 points.
The buck was killed on November 29, 1971, in Oglethorpe County.

NONTYPICAL RACK
No entries.
*This category has been discontinued from the contest.

WEIGHT
J. W. Plemmons of Griffin, Ga.—304 lb. 7 oz.
This buck was killed November 27, 1971, in Spalding County.

STATE RECORDS

Typical Rack: 184 pts., Gene Almand, Riverdale, Newton County, November 16, 1966.

Nontypical Rack: 197 3/8 pts., R. H. Bumbalough, Stone Mountain, Newton County, November 1, 1969.

Weight: 320 lbs., Barry Hancock, Thomaston, Upson County, November 4, 1967.

RULES:

1. Any hunter is eligible regardless of whether or not he is a member of an affiliated club of the Georgia Sportsman's Federation or a subscriber to Outdoors in Georgia Magazine. Hunters need not be residents of the State of Georgia to enter, but only deer taken in the State of Georgia by legal means and in conformity with all state and federal game laws and regulations may be entered.

2. Only deer killed during the current season will be considered for the contest prizes.

3. Deer killed with a bow and arrow are also eligible, provided they meet minimum requirements. Indicate that archery equipment was used, rather than a rifle or shotgun.

4. PHOTOGRAPH: A clear photograph is desirable if it's one that can be kept by Outdoors in Georgia Magazine. Please do NOT send a photograph that you want returned. All photographs and entry forms become the property of Outdoors in Georgia Magazine. Please identify all pictures submitted with your name written on the back.

5. The Georgia Sportsman's Federation and Outdoors in Georgia Magazine reserve the right to re-measure any trophy rack entered, to interview witnesses of kill date and to refuse any questionable application.

6. Before the affidavit can be accepted, the truth of the statements must be attested before a qualified officer such as a notary public, justice of the peace, sheriff, municipal clerk, postmaster, member of a state or local law enforcement agency, wildlife ranger, etc.

7. There is no entry fee for the contest.

8. Split or repaired skulls will not be accepted.

9. Antlers may not show removed or repaired points. Bucks entered as trophy racks need not be weighed.

10. All antlers must air dry for 60 days before measurements can be taken. Each applicant must present to the measurer an affidavit noting date of kill.

11. Address all correspondence regarding these awards to: Big Deer Contest, Outdoors In Georgia Magazine, 270 Washington St., S.W., Atlanta, Georgia 30334. Deadline for entries is June 1, 1973.

VERIFYING OFFICIALS

NORTHWEST
William C. Collins
Game Mgt. Reg. Headquarters
Rt. 1
Armuchee, Ga.
404/232-9711 or 232-9712

NORTHEAST
James Scharnagel
Rt. 2
Gainesville, Ga. 30501
404/536-9936

CENTRAL
Richard Whittington
Rt. 3, Box 7A
Ft. Valley, Ga. 31030
912/825-8248

SOUTH CENTRAL
Frank Parrish
Rt. 1
Fitzgerald, Ga. 31750
912/423-2988

SOUTHWEST
Oscar Dewberry
P.O. Box 911
Bainbridge, Ga. 31717
912/246-8610

COASTAL
C. V. Waters
Sapelo Island, Ga. 31327
912/485-2481

Georgiology

By Allen R. Coggins

Panola Mountain

Millions of years ago great movements within the earth pushed up the present Appalachian Mountains. This process did not happen in a single year or even in a thousand years, but ever so slowly as illustrated above in the writing of Wyckoff. As the mountains were born, the elements of wind and water, ice and gravity slowly began to wear them down by erosion.

Some sections of the Appalachians have eroded more rapidly than others. In the southern part of the chain resistant granite rock exposiers have persisted as remnants of once greater mountains. These are now lost to the great destroyer, time. Several of these rock exposiers (or outcrops) are present today in the vicinity of Atlanta. Being prominent features of the landscape, their names are familiar to

17

Photo by Bob Busby

many Georgians: Stone Mountain, Mount Arabia, Rock Chapel Mountain, Mount Rollaway, and Panola Mountain.

The latter is perhaps the most important of these granite mountains from the standpoint of its unspoiled nature. Panola Mountain is a recent addition to the Georgia State Parks System. It has not been subjected to grazing, quarrying, garbage dumping, recreational usage or any of the other adverse activities which have all but destroyed the primitive nature of other such areas.

This mountain is located about eighteen miles southeast of Atlanta on the southwest end of Rockdale County and adjacent to Henry and DeKalb Counties. The Atlanta skyline is visible on clear days toward the north-

west, although as of late, clear days are few and far between.

This park, is expected to be open to the public by the summer of 1973. At this time the area is restricted and patrolled by a security officer. Because of its delicate nature, Panola mountain cannot withstand the pressure of public visitation until some protective measures are completed. These will include trails and raised walkways.

For thirty years, Panola Mountain was under the ownership of a reclusive family known as the Yarboroughs. They used the mountain and its surrounding fields and forests as a private retreat. Their land was posted and no one except close friends were allowed on the property. In mid-1968, the property was put up for sale. Realizing its value as the last remaining un-

spoiled area of its kind in the state, the Nature Conservancy acquired it. In July of 1970 the Georgia Conservancy took over ownership and shortly thereafter deeded it to the state. On May 10, 1971 Panola became a state park.

The funds necessary for the purchase of Panola were obtained on a matching basis by the State of Georgia

Photo by Bob Wilson

18

and the United States Department of the Interior, Bureau of Outdoor Recreation.

The unique quality of Panola Mountain was realized long before the state acquired it. It is the only large, elevated outcropping of granite in the state which remains unspoiled by man. Furthermore, it is also the abode of several rare plants and animals. Some species found there are present nowhere else in the world, save a few other nearby granite outcrops. Although these other outcrops are now threatened by encroaching civilization, Panola will be protected in its natural state for all times.

The endemic species at Panola are specially adapted for living under adverse conditions. Such conditions include heavy wind, pounding rain, and ice as well as extremes of heat and cold. The only protection the plants have is their ability to thrive and reproduce when conditions are good and lie dormant when conditions are not good. Many complete their life cycles in the early and mid-spring when moisture is abundant. The very existence of all the plants and animals on Panola is dependent upon how well the Parks and Recreation Division maintains the natural state of the area. The state is faced with the problem of keeping it natural while still allowing public access.

The hundred-acre lichen and moss-covered mountain, for which the park was named, contains many saucer or bowl-shaped depressions called "solution pits." This harbor a very thin layer of mineral soil and varying complexities of vegetation. Some are small and contain a single plant species called Diamorpha. Other larger depressions contain mosses, lichens and flowering plants as well as deeper soil. These depressions, being older, have had time to collect greater amounts of decaying organic matter. Still other solution pits have shrubs and trees in addition to the lower plants. Trees have been able to survive due to greater soil buildup in the larger depressions. When walking from the summit to the base of Panola Mountain, one can actually see in this small area a recording of the process of evolution from a billion years ago to the present. This makes the mountain an excellent place in which to study the dynamics and balances of the natural world. The original dry land surface of primitive earth was probably much like Panola's seemingly barren face is today. Moving from lichen and moss-covered granite into one of the depressions, soil becomes deeper, and moisture conditions became more favorable. The result is a concurrent increasing complexity of plant and animal life. This same process has occurred over a period of millions of years on a world-wide scale. It is therefore possible, to a degree, to gain an understanding of the development of the more complex forms of life on earth through a study of the mountain.

Within a short distance of Panola, one can find old farm fields in various stages of abandonment and young maturing hardwood and pine forests. Add to this a two acre lake, several streams and a few additional minor granite outcrops, and you have a very diverse, rich and beautiful area for research, nature study, sight seeing and other activities of a passive type.

The Park Service statement of purpose for Panola Mountain reads:

Panola Mountain State Park has been created by the Georgia Department of Natural Resources, Parks and Recreation Division for the purpose of protecting for all times the area's unique features; for the interpretation of its significance in terms of natural history and ecology; for its utilization in research and public environmental education and for public recreation, oriented toward a better understanding, appreciation and enjoyment of the natural environment.

This statement was drafted jointly by a special Panola Mountain Advisory Committee in January of 1972. This group was made up of scientists, educational consultants, representatives of the Georgia Department of Natural Resources and a planning firm (Environmental Planning and Engineering of Atlanta). The advisory committee was set up to determine how best to develop this unique park while least affecting its natural characteristics. This was done during the development of the master plan so that certain deterrents to over-use and abuse might be built into the plan.

It was determined that if the delicate ecological balance at Panola was to be maintained, only minimal development could be permitted in and around the mountain. Hard-surface access trails, overlooks, and other public safety features are all that will

Photo by Paul Karchak

be developed throughout most of the park.

Picnic tables, parking, maintenance area, personnel residences, visitor information center and rest room facilities will be developed in a fifty acre area on the south end of the park adjacent to State Highway 155. The remaining 421 acres, the natural area, will be entirely fenced.

Georgia is fortunate indeed to have an area like Panola only 20 minutes away from its capitol city. This park will preserve the untold generations of wild things that will be born and die there from this time forward. Man will remain but a visitor to the area, and a welcomed guest as long as he continues to respect the ways of the wild and does not interfere. Man has conquered most of the earth's surface, so let him dwell in his places, improve upon them, change them to fit his moods. But let him not decide the destiny of even the least creature within the few natural preserves which we have left. We hope that the natural things within areas like Panola will be given the inalienable rights to which man himself aspires, to be born, to live free and to die a noble death in the way that nature sees fit.

Quail Habits & Habitats

By Aaron Pass

BUSINESS REPLY MAIL

NO POSTAGE STAMP NECESSARY IF MAILED IN THE UNITED STATES

Postage will be paid by

Department of Natural Resources

270 WASHINGTON STREET, S.W.

ATLANTA, GEORGIA 30334

First Class
Permit No. 5091
Atlanta, Ga.

Whenever and wherever quail hunters gather to swap guns, dogs and lies, the continuing decline in the quality of quail hunting is a much discussed topic. Amid the pleasantries of evaluating the merits of "best-grade" Parkers as opposed to English guns or speculation on the retrieving proficiency of pointers vs. setters, there comes the inevitable lament that, "Quail hunting isn't what it used to be." This sad song is most often sung by hunters on the wrong side of middle age, who have a tendency to remember the good old days with more nostalgia than accuracy.

There are a number of verses to this mournful dirge all of which painfully recount how quail and quail hunting has changed for the worse. Instead of holding patiently for a pointing dog, the birds now run like thieves or flush wild, long before man or dog get anywhere near. When a covey is found it will almost always be in or near the most inaccessible tangle of briar, honeysuckle, and muscadine vines anywhere in sight. On the flush, the birds can be counted on to roar into the nearest pine thicket. Instead of the leisurely doubles one used to make in open fallow fields, the hunter must now settle for a rushed snapshot at his target before it is enveloped in the greenery. Once in the thicket, the birds may perch in the trees or land running on the ground. If the hunter follows them into the jungle, he will be mainly rewarded by the sound of the single flushing beyond the intervening pines.

Those birds which are brought to bag seem smaller and lighter in color than the quail our hunter remembers from the "good old days." Finally, and most horrible of all, quail seem to be getting scarce. A day's hunt that used to produce 5 or 6 flushes is now very good if 4 coveys are seen. To the dedicated quail hunter such a situation borders on the intolerable.

"Dedicated" is what the southern quail hunter is all about. The natural range of the bobwhite quail may go as far north as Wisconsin and west to eastern Colorado, but only in the southeast does this small brown bird command such a zealous following of hunters. This situation partially exists because the bobwhite quail is the only resident game bird which is present in

any significant number in this region. Quail are so dominant as a game species that to go bird hunting in the south is to go quail hunting.

Another factor has to do with the history and traditions that surround quail hunting. In the heyday of southern "bird shooting," the aristocracy hunted quail from specially constructed shooting carts drawn by a team of matched mules, and behind braces of the finest bird dogs their money could buy. The less affluent hunted on foot but with no less enthusiasm and likewise had the best dogs **their** money could buy. These were the days of the agrarian South; cotton was king and was grown on the large plantations as well as the small farms. Farming was the mainstay of the economy and most men, rich and poor, were farmers. Quail were plentiful and most hunters were "bird hunters." Matters of great importance were discussed on many of these hunts. Stock and land was traded, marriages were arranged, and many a politician was made just south of the mules which pulled the "quail wagon." Consequently, the bobwhite quail is not only a great little game bird of sterling sporting quality, but is also a tangible link with some of the most hallowed and romantic aspects of southern heritage and culture.

It is not surprising that an all too noticeable decline in the quality of quail hunting is of serious concern to a large number of southern hunters. Neither is it surprising that this problem became one of paramount interest to the game departments in the southern states. For the past ten or fifteen years a great deal of intensive research has been directed toward finding the reasons for and hopefully stopping the quail decline. The reasons were not very difficult to isolate; the replacement of a small farm economy with the agri-business complex, a rural to urban population shift, and the subsequent changes in land-use have been detrimental to quail. The prognosis is not very cheerful. The decline may be slowed or in some instances even stopped by specific and intensive quail management, but quail hunting as it used to exist in the south is gone with the wind of change.

Before we go any further with the current difficulties of the quail population, let us discuss the history and origins of our main character, the bob-

white quail **(Colinus virgianus).** This sturdy little gentleman, named for his cheery, two-note whistle, has been around in basic form for about 1,000,-000 years. The early southern Indians certainly utilized the quail for food but did not consider it a staple. They preferred the more filling turkey and deer which were numerous in the vast forest which covered eastern America. From all reports of the earliest travelers, these original quail populations were scattered and spotty, existing mostly near the small fields cultivated by the Indians or large natural openings. These same habitat requirements have now, in modern times, once again become a significant limiting factor on quail populations.

The quail family is a member of the Gallinaceous order of birds, an order which includes grouse, pheasant and partridge. Quail, like all galliformes, spend most of their time on the ground and feed mostly on small plant seeds, vegetable matter and insects. Insects are particularly needed by the young birds for protein during the chicks' growth months of spring and summer. Quail favor habitat that is open or only slightly brushy where weed or grain seeds are abundant and there is nearby brush for nesting and protection from predators. Quail will scratch for food but are not powerful, and ground litter, if present at all, must be light. With these requirements it is understandable that quail were originally limited to scattered forest openings where grass seeds and insects were available.

There are three unyielding requirements for quail habitat: food, water and cover. Water supply in the southeast is adequate in most instances and has changed little over the years. The quail food and cover supply has been more variable and these have historically been the major limiting factors. Both factors are the results of "disruptive ecology" which breaks up the canopy of a maturing forest and allows sunlight to reach the forest floor. This encourages the growth of seed-bearing weeds and grasses which furnish quail abundant food and cover. The first major contribution to the bobwhite quail was made by the first European settlers to the new world.

With the coming of the white man, the whole eastern landscape began to change and so too did the habitat of the quail. The first settlers were hard pressed to hack tiny clearings in the forest and to plant their sustenance crops. They managed, however, and were followed by more settlers who made similar clearings. With each clearing in the forest, quail habitat increased.

This trend continued into the early 1900's when the formerly vast eastern hardwood forest was almost completely replaced by farmland. The wild turkey and other forest game had dwindled, but the quail populations were blossoming. In the south, King Cotton reigned and while cotton contributed little directly to the quail, the brushy field borders and creek bottoms were good habitat. The small farmer also found it necessary to raise his own garden and grain for his stock and the waste from these crops was a direct benefit to the quail. All cultivation was accomplished by man and mule-power and as a consequence there was usually a good number of spots that were infeasible to tend. These brushy ravines, fence corners, and spring heads made ideal escape and nesting cover for the birds.

The Civil War broke up the old plantation system and brought "small farm agriculture" to its peak for the next 60 years. The landscape resembled a patch-work quilt of cotton and grain fields separated by creeks, brushy fallow fields, and woodlots. The diversity of crops grown and the interspersion of escape cover created a quail paradise and there was a marked increase in quail populations during this period.

This quail population explosion lasted until the 1940's over most of the south. It was during these years that Georgia boasted itself as the quail capitol of the world. Rich and famous men journeyed far to take part in the fantastic wingshooting on the great "quail plantations," and still-famous lines of gun dogs rose to prominence. These were the golden days of southern quail shooting and the sport became as much a cultural institution as a recreational pursuit.

The end of World War II might well mark the beginning of the end of these "golden days" for the southern quail hunter. Beginning about this time were a number of profound changes that would eventually sweep the Progressive South. For the next thirty years these changes would alter the population distribution, agricul-

tural practices, and the economic system of the region. They would also alter the habitat of the bobwhite quail. In retrospect we see that most of the land-use changes of the past thirty years have, on the whole, been detrimental to quail, and even in the earliest years a decline of the species was a foregone conclusion.

The most far-reaching change, and one which lies basically at the root of the others, was a widespread shift in population distribution from rural to urban locations. The reasons for this migration were simple enough, more money could be made in the industrializing cities than by farming. The result being, over the years, a net loss in the number of producing farms. Good quail shooting would still be available in the fallow fields around the abandoned farm buildings for a few more years, but this was to fade. The annual weeds gave way to the perennials which were in turn replaced by woody shrubs and seedling trees as the forest reclaimed the land through plant succession.

Quail habitat requirements dictate the availability of weed seeds for food and the presence of brush for cover. Early farming methods provided both in abundance, plus the waste grain from the crops grown which further enhanced the food supply. So directly do quail populations relate to the degree and type of agricultural activity that quail are among those species classed as "farm game" for management purposes.

It would be a vast oversimplification to say that all agricultural practices benefit quail. Quail traditionally thrived best in the presence of the small farm system widely practiced in

the south following the Civil War. This "forty acres and a mule" agriculture was grossly inefficient in comparison to the modern agri-business operation, but it provided well for the needs of quail in terms of interspersion of habitat and provided ample food and cover in close proximity to one another. Modern techniques of farming have added a great deal of efficiency to the production of food and fiber but have decimated the quail habitat, once a by-product of farming. The brushy ravine or fence row and other patches of idle land are apparently a bane to the modern, efficient farm manager, and with modern heavy equipment it is simple enough to do something about them. It is also highly efficient to crop as large a contiguous area as possible. The huge fields are cultivated in carefully rotated monocultures with clean edges and no wasted space. The quail have gone the way of the wasted space.

The advent of cattle ranching has also had a deleterious effect on quail populations. The large, open expanses of grassland provide some seeds for food but no cover from predators, and few quail will venture into such a place.

A growing southern forest industry involved in a whirlwind love affair with pine trees has usurped its share of quail habitat. The urban migration resulted in the reversion of a great deal of farmland to forest land. This trend encouraged the development of the forest industry and the demand for pulp and paper sustained it. The ubiquitous pine tree is the prince of modern scientific forest management because it grows fast, thick, and is readily marketable. Row after row of

The good, the bad, and the ugly. The photos on this page illustrate three concepts of land use which have tremendous bearing on quail populations over the state. The brushy field border in the first picture would look sloppy to an efficient farm manager, but quail call it home. This transitional area between field and forest provides the close association of food and cover vegetation that quail need to survive. The clean, no-waste dairy operation in the second picture has no brushy field borders and a large percentage of the acreage is in unbroken pasture. It is an efficient, sterile habitat that produces few quail. Sterility plus is found under the closed canopy of an even-aged pine stand; no cover and no food for quail or anything else. Under-story growth that quail could utilize is prevented by the dense over-story of tree tops which cut off sunlight and carpet the ground with needles and debris.

even-age pines now stand in closed ranks ready for the pulp mill in what were quail fields thirty years ago. Admittedly, specific and intensive management of pine forest with wildlife values in mind will produce good quail hunting. Such management is somewhat costly, however, and since it does not aid the growing trees, it is seldom practiced.

To add to this tale of gloom, there are yet two more threats to the bobwhite quail of considerably more modern origin. The most sinister of these is the heavy use of persistent pesticides over the past few years. This strikes directly at the vitally important protein diet of insects which is so necessary to young birds in the spring and summer. In some instances, particularly heavy applications of these poisons such as Mirex, have been reported to cause direct mortality to quail and other wildlife.

The second modern problem is, paradoxically, the exact opposite of the original rural-urban population shift. The flight from the cities to the suburbs is now gobbling vast chunks of quail habitat. The leap-frogging sub-divisions being thrown up around most sizeable cities, with their inevitable shopping centers and expressways, not only usurp the land on which they are developed, but the intervening lands as well. These new almost-rural residents did not come back to farm, but only to reside and commute to the city. Thus, around every major city, there has developed a wide band of "no quail's land."

Little wonder then that the old quail hunter bemoans the loss of his quarry, for quail hunting in reality has declined statewide. This has been

a relatively slow process and will continue slowly in the years to come. There are still many isolated spots which provide good hunting and neither the bobwhite quail nor the quail hunter is likely to vanish from Georgia overnight. Quail hunting will only continue to decline in a proportionate degree to the deterioration of the habitat.

It has been and is an imminently natural process which proves empirically the direct interrelationship of wildlife with its environment. As the useable habitat expands, the wildlife population expands to fill it, and as it contracts, the wildlife population will shrink to keep within its bounds. In the case of the bobwhite quail, it is a bird of the open fields with adjacent brush. In the early clearing of the forest the small, independent farmer created ideal quail habitat and the quail responded. It rose with the small farm economy and now is declining with it. As we continue to lose quail habitat, the quail population will continue to stay within these bounds.

23

INDEX•OUTDOORS in GEORGIA · July 1972 to December 1972

Compiled by
Janey Beadles

Sportsman's Calendar

DOVES: December 2 through January 13. Daily shooting hours are from 12 noon until sunset. The daily bag limit is 12 and the possession limit is 24.

DUCKS: December 2 through January 20. Bag limit is 5 daily with the possession limit of 10. Limits on ducks are one black duck daily and two in possession, four mallards daily and eight in possession, and two wood ducks daily and four in possession.

CANVASBACK, REDHEAD DUCKS, BRANT AND GEESE: There is no open season.

COOTS: December 2 through January 20. Bag limit is 15 daily with the possession limit of 20.

FOX: There is no closed season on the taking of fox. It is unlawful for any person to take or attempt to take any fox, within the State, by use or aid of recorded calls or sounds or recorded or electronically amplified imitations of calls or sounds.

GROUSE: October 14 through February 28. Bag limit 3 daily with the possession limit of 6.

WILD HOGS: Hogs are considered non-game animals in Georgia. They are legally the property of the landowner, and cannot be hunted without his permission, except on public lands. Firearms are limited to shotguns with Number 4 shot or smaller, .22 rimfire rifles, centerfire rifles with bore diameter .225 or smaller, all caliber pistols, muzzle loading firearms and bows and arrows.

OPOSSUM: October 16 through February 28 in Carroll, Fulton, DeKalb, Gwinnett, Barrow, Jackson, Madison, Elbert, and all counties north of those listed. No bag limit. Night hunting allowed. All counties south of the above named counties are open year round for the taking of opossum. No

bag limit. Night hunting allowed.

QUAIL: November 20 through February 28. Statewide season. Bag limit 12 daily with the possession limit of 36.

RABBIT: November 20 through January 31 in the counties of Carroll, Fulton, DeKalb, Gwinnett, Hall, Habersham, and all counties north of those listed. Bag limit 5 daily. November 20 through February 28 in all counties south of the above listed counties. Bag limit 10 daily.

RACCOON: October 16 through February 28 in Carroll, Fulton, DeKalb, Gwinnett, Barrow, Jackson, Madison, Elbert and all counties north of those listed. Bag limit 1 per night per person. Night hunting allowed. All counties south of the above named counties are open year round for the taking of raccoons. No bag limit. Night hunting allowed.

SQUIRREL: November 4 through February 28. Bag limit 10 daily.

TURKEY: November 20 through February 28 in Baker, Calhoun, Decatur, Dougherty, Early, Grady, Miller, Mitchell, Seminole, Thomas Counties. Bag limit 2 per year.

Book Review

A HUNTER'S FIRESIDE BOOK
By Gene Hill, Winchester Press. 162 pages, $7.95.

If the hunter in your family is a problem when it comes to Christmas gifts, this book might be a solution. It is almost guaranteed to please any hunter since it is all about himself and what he thinks and feels for his sport. "The Fireside Book" is a collection of short stories, anecdotes and reflections on hunters and hunting by Gene Hill, writer of the "Tail Feathers" column in *Sports Afield*.

The subject matter of the book ranges so wide as to defy classification and categorization. Including such titles as, The Perfect Gun, The Perfect Woman, The High Sierras, Optimism and Culture, it is obvious this book covers vast territory. It is a funny-sad book, deep and trivial, so paradoxical that chapters on "Collecting Guns" and "Saving Your Marriage" are separated only by a brief anecdote on "Feeling Guilty."

Delving deeply into the motivations which spur hunters to hunt, the book is saved from its philosophical bent by a practical how-to chapter on sneaking another new gun into the house. A hunter can laugh at an imaginary trip with a migrating woodcock and understand the grief over the death of a promising puppy who had been around long enough to select a certain corner by the stove.

Hill writes also about the homely little things like wet boots drying by the fire, mail order catalogs from sporting goods stores, and friends who outshoot him but whom he likes anyway. The significance is not in the topics selected but in the manner in which the tales are told. The prose is simple and direct, drawing lovely, lingering images of these common things in the hunter's world.

Author Hill is obviously a hunter, for no one but a hunter could feel the things he feels. He is also a writer of rare skill and perception for only a gifted writer could express those feelings so perfectly. Hill captures those minute details and fleeting moments that, while not large in the big picture, are the essence and texture of the never ending game of chase the hunter plays with his game and life itself.

The Hunter's Fireside Book is aptly named since it warms the hunter's soul as the fire warms his body. Best of all, it costs less than a good load of firewood.

—AFP

ARCHERY, FROM GOLDS TO BIG GAME by Keith C. Schuyler, A. S. Barnes & Co., Inc., Cranbury, New Jersey. 569 pages, $12.00.

Keith Schuyler has been an archer for more than 30 years. His experience and knowledge of the sport help to make this book a fine contribution to available archery literature.

It is an attempt to cover all aspects of archery from selection of tackle through target competition to hunting both small and big game.

It is a book that will fit well into any archer's library but is of special interest to the beginner because of the detailed discussion of competitive archery rounds, advantages and disadvantages of certain types of tackle, basic hunting methods and a review of organized archery.

There is a chapter on archery safety that should be read by novices and experienced archers alike.

Schuyler's discussions of the history of archery and common terms originating in archery make interesting reading. The author's discussion of hunting techniques will be of interest to experienced archers as well as beginners. The book is illustrated with more than 250 photos.

—Marvin Tye

Lightning Source UK Ltd.
Milton Keynes UK
UKHW020642110119

335238UK00006B/67/P